THIS BOOK BELONGS TO

children's
choice®

BEDTIME
FOR FRANCES

by RUSSELL HOBAN

Pictures by GARTH WILLIAMS

HARPER & ROW, PUBLISHERS
New York, Evanston, and London

A Children's Choice® Book Club Edition From Scholastic Book Services

BEDTIME FOR FRANCES
Text copyright © 1960 by Russell C. Hoban
Pictures copyright © 1960 by Garth Williams
Printed in the United States of America
All rights in this book are reserved.
Library of Congress catalog card number: 60-8347

Trade Standard Book Number 06-022350-2
Harpercrest Standard Book Number 06-022351-0

This one is for Ursula.

The big hand of the clock is at 12.
The little hand is at 7.
It is seven o'clock.
It is bedtime for Frances.
Mother said, "It is time for bed."
Father said, "It is time for bed."
Frances said, "I want a glass of milk."
"All right," said Father.
"All right," said Mother.
"You may have a glass of milk."
Frances drank the milk.

"Carry me to my room, Father," said Frances.

"All right," said Father.

"Piggyback," said Frances.

So Father carried her piggyback to her room.

Father kissed Frances good night.

Mother kissed Frances good night.

Frances said, "May I sleep with my teddy bear?"

Father gave her the teddy bear.

Frances said, "May I sleep with my doll, too?"

Mother gave her the doll.

"Good night," said Father.

"Good night," said Mother.

"Did you kiss me?" said Frances.

"Yes," said Mother.

"Yes," said Father.

"Kiss me again," said Frances.

Father kissed her again.

Mother kissed her again.

They closed the door.

"May I have my door open?" said Frances.

Father opened the door.

"Good night," said Mother.

"Good night," said Father.

"Good night," said Frances.

Frances could not sleep.

She closed her eyes, but she still could not sleep.

So she began to sing a little song about the alphabet.

She made it up as she went along:

"A is for apple pie,
B is for bear,
C is for crocodile, combing his hair.
D is for dumplings . . ."
Frances kept singing through E, F, G, H, I, J, K, L, M, N, O,
P, Q, and R, and she had no trouble until
she got near the end of the alphabet.

"S is for sailboat,
T is for tiger,
U is for underwear, down in the drier..."
Frances stopped because "drier" did not sound like "tiger."
She started to think about tigers.
She thought about big tigers and little tigers,
baby tigers and mother and father tigers,
sister tigers and brother tigers,
aunt tigers and uncle tigers.
"I wonder if there are any tigers around here," she said.
Frances looked around her room.
She thought maybe she could see a tiger in the corner.
She was not afraid, but she wanted to be sure.

So she looked again.
She was sure she could see a tiger.
She went to tell Mother and Father.
"There is a tiger in my room," said Frances.
"Did he bite you?" said Father.
"No," said Frances.
"Did he scratch you?" said Mother.
"No," said Frances.
"Then he is a friendly tiger," said Father.
"He will not hurt you. Go back to sleep."
"Do I have to?" said Frances.
"Yes," said Father.
"Yes," said Mother.

Father kissed her.
Mother kissed her.
Frances went back to bed, and finished her song on the way.
She closed her eyes again.
She still could not sleep.
Frances opened her eyes and looked around.

She saw something big and dark.
"Giants are big and dark," she thought.
"Maybe that is a giant.
I think it *is* a giant.
I think that giant wants to get me."
She went into the living room.

Mother and Father were watching television
and having tea and cake.
Frances said, "There is a giant in my room.
May I watch television?"
"No," said Mother.
"No," said Father.
Frances said, "The giant wants to get me.
May I have some cake?"
Father gave Frances a piece of cake.
Father said, "How do you know he wants to get you?"
Frances said, "Isn't that what giants do?"
Father said, "Not always. Why don't you ask him what he wants?"
Frances went back to her room.
She went right over to the giant.
She said, "What do you want, Giant?"

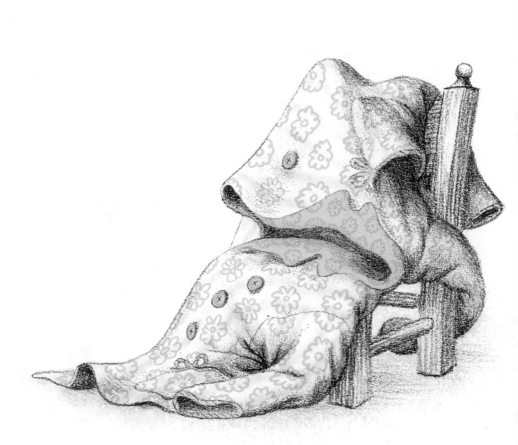

She took a good look at him.
There was no giant.
It was just the chair and her bathrobe.
So she went to bed again.
Frances was not very tired and did not close her eyes.
She looked up at the ceiling.
There was a crack in the ceiling, and she thought about it.

"Maybe something will come out of that crack," she thought.
"Maybe bugs or spiders. Maybe something with a lot of skinny
legs in the dark."

She went to get Father. He was brushing his teeth.
Frances said, "Something scary is going to come out of
the crack in the ceiling. I forgot to brush my teeth."
Father said, "You brush your teeth, and I will have a look."

Frances brushed her teeth.
Father came back and said, "Nothing could come out of such a little crack. But if you are worried about it, get somebody to help you watch. You can take turns."

Frances told her teddy bear to watch.
They took turns for a while.
Then Frances got tired of it and let Teddy do all the watching.
Frances got up and went to the bathroom.
When she came back she was not sleepy at all.
The window was open and the wind was blowing the curtains.

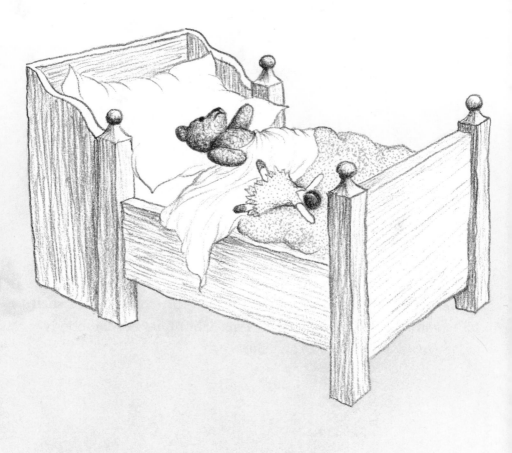

"I do not like the way those curtains are moving,"
said Frances.
"Maybe there is *something* waiting, very soft and quiet.
Maybe it moves the curtains just to see if I am watching."
She went into Mother and Father's room to tell them.

They were asleep.

Frances stood by Father's side of the bed very quietly, right near his head.

She was so quiet that she was the quietest thing in the room.

She was so quiet that Father woke up all of a sudden, with his eyes wide open.

He said, "Umph!"

Frances said, "There is something moving the curtains. May I sleep with you?"

Father said, "Listen, Frances, do you want to know why the curtains are moving?"

"Why?" said Frances.

"That is the wind's job," said Father. "Every night the wind has to go around and blow all the curtains."

"How can the wind have a job?" said Frances.

"*Everybody* has a job," said Father.
"I have to go to my office every morning at nine o'clock.
That is my job. You have to go to sleep
so you can be wide awake for school tomorrow.
That is *your* job."
Frances said, "I know, but . . ."
Father said, "I have not finished.
If the wind does not blow the curtains, he will be out of a job.
If I do not go to the office, I will be out of a job.
And if you do not go to sleep now,
do you know what will happen to you?"
"I will be out of a job?" said Frances.
"No," said Father.
"I will get a spanking?" said Frances.
"Right!" said Father.

"Good night!" said Frances, and she went back to her room.
Frances closed the window and got into bed.
Suddenly there was a noise at the window.
She heard BUMP! and THUMP!
"I *know* something will get me this time," she thought.

She jumped out of bed and went to tell Mother and Father.
When she got to their door, she thought about it some more
and decided not to tell them.
She went back to her room.
Frances heard the noise at the window again.
She pulled the covers over her head.
"I wonder what it is," she thought.

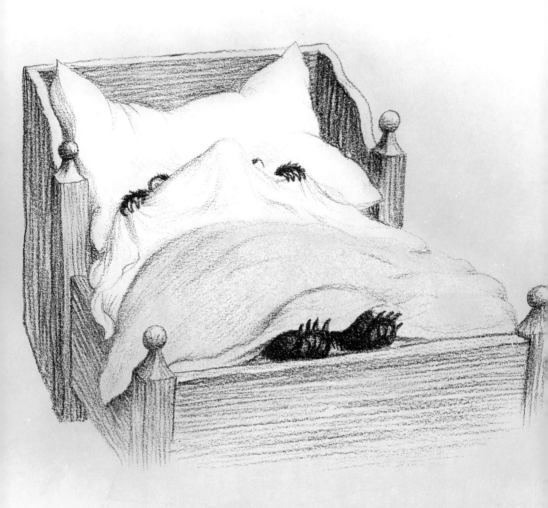

"If it is something *very* bad, Father will *have* to come
and chase it away."
She pulled off the covers and stood on her bed
so she could look out the window.
She saw a moth bumping against the window.

Bump and thump.
His wings smacked the glass.
Whack and smack!
Whack and smack made Frances think of a spanking.
And all of a sudden she was tired.
She lay down and closed her eyes
so she could think better. She thought,
"There were so many giants and tigers
and scary and exciting things before,
that I am pretty tired now.
That is just a moth, and he is only doing his job,
the same as the wind.
His job is bumping and thumping,
and my job is to sleep."
So she went to sleep
and did not get out of bed again
until Mother called her for breakfast.